YOU MADE A WAY WHEN THERE WAS NO WAY

Tod Trader
You Made A Way When There Was No Way

Published by BooxAi
ISBN: 978-965-577-932-5

YOU MADE A WAY WHEN THERE WAS NO WAY

LESSONS FROM LIFE'S GREATEST MOTIVATIONAL TEACHER

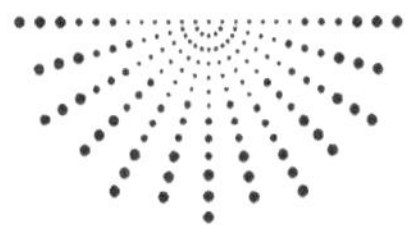

TOD TRADER

CONTENTS

1. Acknowledgment   7
2. In the beginning   11
3. Revision   19
4. God The Father   23
5. Prayer   39
6. Faith   53
7. States   59
8. Struggling with the law   65

ACKNOWLEDGMENT

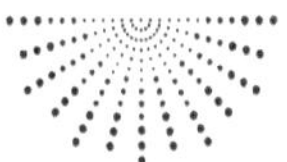

There are many I could thank that have helped develop me into me throughout my lifetime. When I say "develop" of course, I'm interpreting how God used them to shape me and ultimately wake me from my slumber. I see they are all gifts to me from God. I as well pray that I can equally be a gift unto them.

Dakota Renee, you are my life. I found mine raising you while you were teaching me always to be better because you could look up and see me. Without you, I wouldn't have learned to enjoy this opportunity called life.

I want to express some of my deepest gratitude to my wife Ximena. I have had, and I can say, enjoyed and regretted many experiences throughout my life well before meeting you and after meeting you. You, my love, were the most challenging and ultimately the most rewarding to the recognition and development of my human existence. I am grateful we came together by divine intervention. I have caused both of us, but I do admit I caused you a lot of pain and hardship. I now understand God used you to call me into service. The person of this world has regret, but my Spirit understands it all played out as divinely scripted. It was all results from the State we occupied.

These moments have been a service for God's kingdom and glory. I now see by my answered prayers you are my divinely appointed mate. I am forever remorseful as the man who caused us both such pain, but I am grateful he used you, used us, to awaken to his calling upon me. To receive his grace and mercy. To share individually, and as a couple, we were able to experience his Glory.

I love you and again am grateful for your strength and ability to forgive. Forgiveness is a difficult trait for many. Maybe because many times it involves acceptance of our own role and responsibility in what we are forgiving for. I thank you for being the catalyst God used to speak directly to me. It is true, the shepherd leaves his flock to find that one lost sheep. During this, he found you and me, and we found each other…again.

I love you more than words can ever say, Ximena. Thank you for giving me and giving the world my experience with God. God does work in ways we do not know.

For the cover art, I want to thank Sanntiago Bernal. I've seen this work that blossomed from within you as an adolescent. I'm grateful for your permission to share it now publicly.

Not that I was ever in need, for I have learned how to be content with whatever I have. I know how to live on almost nothing or with everything. I have learned the secret of living in every situation, whether it's with a full stomach or empty, with plenty or with little. For I can do everything through Christ, who gives me strength.

Philippians 4:11-13 (NLT)

2

IN THE BEGINNING

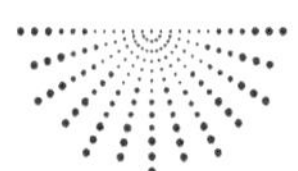

I wouldn't have written this information if I didn't believe through my own testing and application. Proving the power time and time again. What I tell you, I am not embarrassed or ashamed. When God called on me, he brought me to a place where only he could speak to me. Metaphorically my burning bush of instruction. Let me say though it didn't feel like it while I was going through my fire, it is true, I was led. I was refined of my impurities. I died to who I was and I was resurrected into another mental State, and grateful to be resurrected, again and again.

> *Indeed, we felt that we had received the sentence of death. But that was to make us rely not on ourselves but on God who raises the dead.*
>
> 2 Corinthians 1:9 (ESV)

There will be people that will ridicule and claim me to be somebody I am not. These people, I can assure you, have not proven one way or another what you are about to read and learn. I urge you, the reader, to prove unto yourself this power you are to consider and apply through love.

I am open to all dialogues, negative or positive. I will only receive those into my thoughts that are in love, as I have no desire to plant seeds that will not bear fruit. My goal is to share this great power that has been revealed to me, that belongs to us all.

For if you love those who love you, what reward do you have? Do not even the tax collectors do the same? And if you greet only your brothers, what more are you doing than others? Do not even the Gentiles do the same? You therefore must be perfect, as your heavenly Father is perfect.

Matthew 5:46-48 (KJV)

"You, therefore, must be perfect, as your heavenly Father is perfect" was revealed to me, Not "I" as in therefore you, BUT everyone is created perfect for God and his will. Even if you are not fulfilling the plans, he has for you as you want to receive. You are fulfilling his plans. To place myself above all in interpreting "you" as "I" is judging another. This only goes against the Will of God. This only binds me to thoughts that have no meaning.

Yes, this power and the law every man is under and can direct because it is always in use. Everyone uses it continually. Consciously and subconsciously. The power and the law are always in action. What we reap, we shall sow. What we tell ourselves is the Word of God and goes out and it will not return void.

So shall my word be that goeth forth out of my mouth: it shall not return unto me void, but it shall accomplish that which I please, and it shall prosper in the thing whereto I sent it.

Isaiah 55:11

Notice I underlined "thing", your word will accomplish equally good, the bad or evil as it needs to be seen as how you send the word out. Abundance of all things comes in all forms. You name it and there is an abundance. Good, evil, sunshine, rain, and the greatest is love.

Guard your thoughts, protect your heart and love. Do all in love. Love is not wanting or bringing harm to your fellow "man." Whatever you desire for yourself or others should not harm another. God does allow wrongdoing. God does allow harm. God does allow evil. God delivers it. God is no respecter of man. God is God. God will do your bidding in any form or action and will deliver upon man, from man. Again God's word is not mocked. It will return, not void.

I form the light, and create darkness: I make peace, and create evil: I the LORD do all these things.

Isaiah 45:7

I don't expect you to trust me. I'm just a messenger. I hope this resonates with all who take the time to read. I really hope it reaches those that are lost in brokenness. Who feel powerless for the destiny of their own lives.

We all need and crave that touch from our healer, our Savior Jesus Christ. Jesus is here to save you. You're told to believe Jesus is saving you; it's for salvation into Heaven and to be with God for eternity. I tell you, through Christ himself, it's for your salvation in all things. Heaven is within you. So Heaven is on earth....take heed, hell is as well. That's our ultimate Free Will. Choosing one over the other. It's completely up to you, free will, your needs, and desires. Financially, health and disease, relationships, protection of our loved ones, it doesn't matter what your need OR desire is. Through love and the desires given by God, it's your salvation. Through your own wants can easily lead to evil and that's your damnation.

Do you want to be with Jesus Christ? Do you want him to go out and prepare a place for you and your desires? You must understand and grasp that he already does. Jesus is continually bringing you to what you express in your mind. Again God is no respecter of man. God is a creator. Thus, you are the creator. Your creating abilities are drawn from God.

Let your heart not be troubled: ye believe in God, believe also in me. In my Fathers house are many mansions: if it were not so, I would have told you. I go to prepare a place for you, I will come again, and receive you unto myself: that where I am, there ye be also. And whither I go ye kow, and the way ye know.

John 14:1 (KJV)

Mansions are states of mind. You can't live in a different state or mansion while occupying the one you are in. If you believe you are poor, you are. If you believe nobody can love you, nobody will show you the love you desire. If you believe you are successful, you will have success. These thoughts of ourselves are our mansions. Jesus does go and prepare a place for you. Jesus aligned all that justifies to you, everything in the state or mansion you do now occupy.

To occupy a new state of mind or mansion. You must first die to the current state of mind. It is more than just thinking about what you desire. It is all about thinking from which you desire. To think about it is nothing more than a daydream. To think from this desire is all faith.

To die to the state of mind is to stop looking at what the eye can see, what your emotions tell you are real, and what others tell you that you once wanted to hear. Listen, even when we hear the words and reactions of others, we may not like them, but we accept, we hear, we think about, and we react upon…continually. A habitual cycle. Die to this. Don't look back.

…and he overthrew those cities, and all the inhabitants of the cities, and that which grew upon the ground. But his wife looked back from behind him, and she became a pillar of salt.

Genesis 19:25-26 (KJV)

When the Bible was written, salt had been and continued for more than a thousand years as the way to preserve food. Salt's ability to preserve food is a founding contributor to the development of civilization.

When I read and began to understand this passage, it became clear to me, Lot's wife could not or would not see the new state of mind as though her husband, Lot had. We can and will dissect this more, but the point I'm getting at, Lot's wife, through her refusal or inability to think from this new state, was preserved in her current state. The state they were trying to escape.

Here is a good reminder the Bible is written, just as Jesus spoke, in parables. The Bible is completely true. Every story written within is hidden only from those unwilling to accept the true teaching that is God. Whom Jesus is. The Bible is absolute power. Many do not grasp the simplicity. The power it has to change you. The power it has to change the world around you. The ancient mystics knew this. They must have known, many more than not, would refuse the responsibility that comes with this power. Thus hiding its meanings and instructions in plain sight.

I've always had the question if God loves me so much, why then do I struggle as much as I have? Why do I always feel powerless? If not powerless in one area, but the feeling of complete lack of any control in other areas of my life. I've been conditioned through religious teaching that I'm lacking in being "good" according to the Bible somewhere, and if not, it's just not God's Will for me.

When I do follow the religious teaching by our or my religious leaders, oh, I'm good…but I now realize "Good for Nothing." Yes, God does instruct us with His Commandments. If I uphold them, the foundation is there to stay in my conscious lane for unpolluted consciousness. When I protect my outer consciousness with God's word, it aligns with my inner consciousness. God. My true and absolute power.

The Bible tells us what to point our outer consciousness for thinking. Understanding our free will, developed by this world, and the bad habits and beliefs cemented by our repeated thoughts and practice will have us to struggle and to question God's word and instruction.

And now, dear brothers and sisters, one final thing. Fix your thoughts on what is true, and honorable, and right, and pure, and lovely, and admirable. Think about things that are excellent and worthy of praise.

Philippians 4:8 (NLT)

Why are we to believe our best life will be after we die? If life is a gift from God, and he loves us, why are we told we can only enjoy the box life comes in…the real enjoyment of the gift of life comes later…when you die. I was trained by this world to believe this is just the way it is….so be good. Good for nothing.

The teaching is always symbolic. When we encounter struggles, difficulties, and problems, we are told to "take it to God." Yet we're never told where we find God other than his scripture. Oh, it's nice symbolism to hear it, take it to the cross and lay it at the feet of Jesus. How could I question that? To question would only prove I'm not a paying attention Christian. I don't know who God is, and the self-condemnation is limitless.

3

REVISION

This will probably be the shortest chapter but one of the most powerful methods to draw closer to God. Consider that in our heads, within our own thoughts, when we begin to take responsibility and quiet the noise, the arguments, our self-destruction, and judgment of ourselves and others which are only a few toxic states. Revision is the power not to change the past that has already been reflected out. Its purpose is to have the power to revise what has already been reflected into what it should be, which is always positive and loving.

Nobody is in your head that you allow but you. You are the one constructing the conversations and events. This revision is free will. This revision I'm talking about happens in our thoughts. Where it matters the most and you are struggling with it now. Doing so changes you. REMEMBER, THE ONLY ONE TO CHANGE IS SELF. Changing self into your desire of how you wanted the outcome, or conversation, or the event to have really happened. You'll feel much better and welcome the needed outcome. So the revision you perform will now live in an elevated state. It is you, the inner man, who is now thinking from and not about living and moving in this elevated State. Many times I find this rearrangement is necessary to be able to augment my faith.

Revision is one of the most powerful ways that helps move quicker into dropping a harmful or unfruitful desire. Revision, through Christ Jesus, brings us directly to our Heavenly Father. Brings healing. I won't tell you it's easy to control your runaway thoughts. We are all guilty of letting bad or unfruitful thoughts claim too much of our day or, worse yet, our weeks, months and years. I'm guilty before revision to have poor thoughts of myself, others, or events. Once you begin to recognize these destructive thoughts, the lengths of their duration will become shorter and shorter.

When you begin to have bad thoughts about anything, you can stop them. Yes, it's just that easy to stop them. The difficulty is in believing the revision you desire. It's only difficult until you marry the revision with feeling. It is equally important to revise and feel how this revision would feel if true. When you can feel how you would feel if the revision is true, then let the thought go. Move on with your day, or if you're practicing revision before sleep, fall off into slumber.

The way I make this transition is by thanking the Father for hearing me, then with my eyes closed, I repeat "I am" while imagining myself walking around in my own skull. I look around like it's a room. I imagine what I see if I were there…and I am. While I say to myself, "I am," I always end with thank you, Father, for hearing me.

> **But Lot's wife looked back as she was following behind him, and she turned into a pillar of salt.**
>
> *Genesis 19:26 (NLT)*

Salt has been a preservative for thousands of years. When I tell you to revise and align with the feeling of how it would feel if true, and now it is where it matters most. Don't look back. Don't preserve yourself in what is not loving or good. Move on into the new State. Allow God to align the path and bring into your life, your new State, the people, experiences, the events necessary to thrive here. Believe you are only passing through. Elevating higher and higher. Transitioning from one State to another. Never look back. Yes, we can remember, but if the memory doesn't serve us in peace, love and joy…revise it.

The revision is not where you're going to struggle.

The struggle is not having the faith in trusting God to lead you. To believe he is the source for all. Do not doubt. The purpose of the revision is to free you from the bondage of self-imprisonment and limitation. Revise, and move towards your desires.

4

GOD THE FATHER

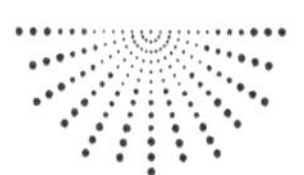

Who is God? What is God? Where is God? All great but simple questions that I'm sure are asked from generation to generation. Let's consider the traditional teaching we currently get from those that "officially" unofficially teach for God. And it appears many of our religious scholars and teachers don't have an answer of God's essence. An answer that fully encapsulates those three questions. I imagine now that when the student is ready, the teacher will appear. Not everyone is ready because it's too easy to conform to our surroundings of this world. What the Bible teaches us not to do.

Do not be conformed to this world, but be transformed by the renewal of your mind, that by testing you may discern what is the Will of God, what is good and acceptable and perfect.

Romans 12:2 (ESV)

Once you know where to find the answers to these questions, you can begin down a narrow path with your relationship with God. It's not narrow in the idea, or assume it must be difficult. No, it's narrow because God is always true. God is always perfect. God is always unwavering. We as men filter everything from our religion, culture, nationality, the color of our skin or the color of others, prejudice, familial beliefs, habits, you name it, and we see it through this worldly filter.

Because strait is the gate, and narrow is the way, which leadeth unto life, and few there be that find it.

Matthew 7:14 (KJV)

We can ask these very similar questions concerning Jesus. Who is Jesus? Where is Jesus? How do I know Jesus? We know because Jesus tells us, ***I am the way, the truth, and the life. No one can come to the Father except through me, you would know who my Father is. From now on, you do know him and have seen him!*** *John 14:6 (NLT)*

So Jesus, from his own word, says we have seen God the Father. Well, now we must ask God to reveal our very 1st question concerning him. We go directly to his word. The 1st time he declared who he was to man was to Moses in Exodus 3:14 (KJV). He said:

I AM THAT I AM

God created you and me in his image. Hence, the power given us in knowing and applying I am that I am. We use this power continually. Believers and nonbelievers alike. There is God's law always and never broken. We have the full life applying his words found in the Bible. We apply this word to ourselves. Not as judgment or leverage to have power or destroy another. We use it to commune with our Father in Heaven. Now, not after this body passes. And apply it to give us power and dominion over this world, sin and hell.

So God created man in his own image, in the image of God He created him; male and female He created them.

Genesis 1:27 (ESV)

Let's move forward and seek answers to the 2nd question, What is God? God is love. God is a creator as he created Heaven and the earth. God is not mocked. God is the truth. When you apply the principle I'll discuss for prayer, always know God is not a respecter of man. Pray in love, love for another. Again that last sentence is very broad. Boil it down to if you want money, for example, and we all do. Money is not a sin. The desire for money is not a sin. Desiring and not fulfilling the achievement of getting the money, that is the sin. Recognize the difference between love and desire. I desire money because it is necessary to commute this flesh through the experience of this world. I recognize what Cesar's, and I render unto Caesar.

They say unto him, Caesar's.
Then saith he unto them, Render therefore unto Caesar the things which are Caesar's; and unto God the things that are God's.

Matthew 22:21

1 John 4:8 ~ Genesis 1:1 ~ Psalm 31:5 (KJV)
He that loveth not knoweth not God; for God is love
In the beginning God created the Heaven and the earth...
Into thine hand I commit my spirit: Thou hast redeemed me, O LORD God of truth.

Now, where is God? Does he live in a cloud? Is he hovering way above us as depicted by others and more so ourselves when we give praise and thanks to God because we always point upwards towards Heaven?

What about Jesus? Where is he? Is he nailed to a cross hung up in our local churches?

Instead of letting man tell us who, what, where and accepting their version. Why don't we let God and Jesus tell us themselves?

I and my Father are one

John 10:30 (KJV)

If I do not the works of my Father, believe me not. But if I do, though ye believe not me, believe the works: that ye may know, and believe the works: that ye may know, and believe, that the Father is in me, and I in him.

John 10:37-38 (KJV)

Do you not know that you are God's temple and that God's Spirit dwells in you?

1 Corinthians 3:16 (ESV)

We are all created by God. Everything in this world is created by God. Everything that is yet to be created has already been and always will be created by God. Time and its reference and or creation are of this world.

For our understanding. Not God's. Every scenario we can imagine is ours for the exercise of faith. If we want to be rich or poor, it already exists. If we want to be a great spouse or just be "married", divorced, happy, or sad, it is ours. It all exists. Our free will and desire will be reflected on this earth.

And he said unto me, "It is done! I am the Alpha and the Omega, the beginning and the end. To the thirsty I will give from the spring of the water of life without payment."

Revelation 21:6 (ESV)

Yes, there are many stories and instances out of our control. These play out, and we question why God would allow it? We must begin to believe God allows everything in this world. Again, God is no respecter of man. God is Spirit, we are Spirit. Our bodies and our flesh are God's Temple and his word for this world, or this reflection for what we call life for the body.

To find God, we only need to go as far as our super-conscious mind. This is where God exists when man calls upon him. His Will, his miracles, his presence. Here we find our creative power. Our healing power. Our power to unite in prayer with and for others.

God is always here. God is always present. God is always listening. God is always speaking to us in his Will. How this life unfolds. It is always by our design, whether we are conscious of this or not. We deny the presence of God by following the ways and lack of understanding of the world. Of man. Just because we deny it doesn't equate God is not present. It matters not if you believe in God or not.

…that ye may be the children of your Father which is in Heaven: for he maketh his sun to rise on the evil and the good, and sendeth rain on the just and unjust.

Matthew 5:45 (KJV)

…neither shall they say, Lo here! Or, lo there! For, behold, the Kingdom of God is within you.

Luke 17:21 (KJV)

The only way to the Father is by Jesus Christ. Jesus and the Father are one. John 10:30 I could write over and over and post scripture. I urge you to read the Bible. Not only to know who God is, but who God says you are. Too much, we are told we are white, or black or Christian, Jewish, Muslim, or of any religious structure. We are told we are American, Mexican, British, Chinese, or of any country of birth. This is not who you are in Christ. This is one of many labels a division man puts on another man. We willfully put limits on ourselves by grouping up.

It all belongs to God. We all belong to God. We are all connected as God. Where you place your thoughts, what mental State, in and of this world, God will bring the connections and the outcomes to answer your conscious prayer. God only supplies in abundance. We are the deciders of what we receive in abundance. Money, sex, love, pain, struggle, opulence, hunger, starvation, peace, war, poverty, being too skinny, being overweight, happy or sad. It's us. It's a choice we make of what we can control. We give up our control to forces outside of us. We make excuses. We blame others. We blame events.

When it's out of our control, as in deformities physical and or mentally, abuse, murder, and accidents. There are countless ways that unspeakable and horrible things happen to mankind, the planet. Then we must find the good in what we witnessed but had no control.

I get it, those last few paragraphs will probably be scrutinized the most. I can accept that. My desire is to follow God. I may not have adequate answers for many of the most troubling and horrific things we do to one another in this world. But, I do know where to go to find my individual answers. I know where to focus in being better unto myself and those that I have influence. I know the answer is not in this world.

The answer is in creating my world within my thoughts. When I attune to my desires. Which our desires are akin to the Word of God. I will always have my prayers answered. The crux you must pay attention to is the desires you have out of love for another. When you focus on these desires and have faith, it is already so, you will receive this desire in action and it will materialize into the world.

Again, the "faith" word. For me, faith was hard to understand until I realized even when I'm not focusing on "faith", my faith is in action. To illustrate, let's assume there is someone you don't want to see because you just don't like who they are. You allow them without consciously being aware of knowing they make you uncomfortable. This is your unwavering "faith" as small as a mustard seed and you don't even recognize it. You've married your thoughts to your feelings. When your paths do eventually cross, well, you are not surprised because you expected the discomfort in the meeting.

This illustration may be too simple to grasp. The illustration is to see how simple "faith" really is in action. Both positively and negatively or toxic. It's your faith. It's your beliefs. You are in control. You are the author. You are the power. You are the blessing or the curse unto yourself and others.

Those that share your mental state, will be ordained to cross your path and interact with you. God is within us all. He moves everyone about to ultimately fulfill his will. We are actors, if you will, in his play of life. What most don't consider is God allows you to write the script, and he will give you the lines to give the best performance for his Glory.

Recognize some of those that don't occupy the same mental state, will cross your path and, at times, interact with you. This is not the moment to look down or up on another. We are equally the same. The beggar in the street is just as valuable as the Pope. The drug addict or the President of The United States are loved and cherished by God equally. Each individual only occupies a different mental state. All are used by God, for God. We just choose the mental state we will occupy. When conscious of our relationship with God and his law, our free will allows us to decide how wonderful, by our definition, our life and encounters are.

Now we know where to find God. How does Jesus bring us to our Father? Where do we find Jesus?

Jesus told him, "I am the way, the truth, and the life. No one can come to the Father except through me. If you had really known me, you would know who my Father is. From now on, you do know him and have seen him!"

John 14:6 (NLT)

Like God our Father, Jesus is always with us. Your consciousness in love and mercy is where you find him. This also is where great miracles and healing are revealed. Jesus responds, exactly like God the Father. Conversely, in the darker realm of Satan, God is there too. It seems never to be admitted or acknowledged, but

God created Satan. However, Satan has power through unloving and hateful means. In every way that is the opposite of God's nature. God is love. God is always with you. Be mindful that if and when we succumb to the desires of Satin, God still fulfills His word. Though it benefits Satin, God's word does not come back void. God produces the good and the bad fruit.

So shall my word be that goes out from my mouth; it shall not return to me empty, but it shall accomplish that which I purpose, and it shall succeed in the thing for which I sent it.

Isaiah 55:11 (ESV)

Jesus is our Savior. Jesus has the power to overcome Satin. Jesus will take your every prayer or desire based on love and manifest it into your spirit. God is the ultimate decider if it will materialize in this world. This revelation of God's materialization matters not to us as we have already received in Spirit. We are Spirit. This is where eternity is found.

When I have a desire. Let's illustrate a desire of mine that has come to pass. It is now evident to those close to me and the world upon inspection. When I occupied a poor man's State of mind, I always was short on money. I always worried about how to fill in the shortages. How to be able to enjoy a better quality life experience. I worried about every bill and was afraid of debt that I felt as though I had no control. I was embarrassed and ashamed.

When God began to awaken me to a deeper understanding of his word. His law. His love, grace and mercy. His promises. Like most, I wanted to believe, but this world and my beliefs kept me skeptical. Over and over again, God would not fail me. When I started to connect the dots, even in my shortcomings and failures. God did not fail me. He delivered me what I unknowingly prayed for through desire, fear, and doubt. He always provided in abundance.

Jesus was always there to rescue me, heal me, provide for me, and comfort me. I realized when I needed anything based or founded in love and envisioned it in my thoughts as finished, at the end result of my desire. When I could feel how this moment in my thoughts, which is as real as you touching your own face, made me feel. It comforted me, it solved my problem, it made me feel good about myself, or made others feel good or lifted them or myself up. When the feeling and the thought married, it was very soon manifested into this world.

I didn't imagine how I would arrive at the desired end result. I just felt myself there. I was thinking from this moment, not about this moment. The details of how is never my concern. God will provide the way. God will provide the necessary people, and God will provide the resources. Remember, it all belongs to him. Any outcome is ours. We have the power to choose, sadly, most don't. But every outcome is there for you. Nothing surprises God. Remember Revelations 21:6. Your free will is the catalyst for the results you receive. Jesus is there in your thoughts of the end results of your desire. Jesus will bring you there.

"Don't let your hearts be troubled. Trust in God, and trust also in me. There is more than enough room in my Father's home. If this were not so, would I have told you that I am going to prepare a place for you? When everything is ready, I will come and get you, so that you will always be with me where I am. And you know the way to where I am going."

John 14:1-4 (NLT)

"My thoughts are nothing like your thoughts," says the Lord. And my ways are far beyond anything you could imagine. For just as the Heavens are higher than earth, so my ways are higher than your ways and my thoughts higher than your thoughts".

Isaiah 55:6-9

I'd be remiss if I didn't acknowledge the role of the Holy Spirit as it has been revealed to me. The Holy Spirit is your heart, the feeling in your gut. He is there to lead and guide. We fail ourselves when we don't follow that gut instinct or our heart's desire. There is a huge and troubling difference between following your heart and your heart's desire.

Our emotions, feelings, and expectations of this world cause our hearts to loudly move us about through this world. The world causes heartbreak, the heart aches. Heart's desire is an instruction from God to follow His Will for our lives. When we do this, we are not worried about riches, finding marriage, health, or academics, and the search list for fulfillment is infinite but never found.

Not everyone is destined for unlimited wealth, health and unshakeable love shared with another human. When we are in agreement with what God speaks to us, we are content and over-filled with a desire to achieve his ultimate plans. What you should know, God doesn't hide his Will from you. God gives you dreams and ambitions that are pursued to bring completeness to our lives on this earth. God doesn't give you these dreams to tease you. God Gives you these dreams to motivate you in testing his law. Don't confuse testing God's law with testing God. Once tested and affirmed, God's laws are his promises in action and fulfillment.

We, as everyone of flesh and blood that is alive upon this earth, are God's children. Children in the definition of what this world calls his. Really we are of his Spirit. Everyone of us is connected. Not just those living today, but those that have passed long before us and those waiting their turn to experience this so-called life. Everyone of us has an ultimate part to play, intertwined and affecting the ultimate path to God's divine plan of eternity.

The Bible is hidden out in the open of parables. An instruction of mastering this life. Many more will not find the true meaning. This is by design, I'm sure, as Adam and Eve were ultimately kicked out of Eden for not following instructions. Now we are destined to search for the meaning as we walk in the flesh of this earth.

I don't believe we all won't be formed again as one Spirit of God at the end of eternity. I believe we all are his. We all had a purpose. We all performed as God wanted from the perspective of this world he created. Where we failed and sinned was not following through on our desires. Good or bad, we all have desires left not only unfulfilled, but we didn't trust God, Jesus, and The Holy Spirit enough to prove we could not have failed.

Get into God's written word and discover the promises. The truth. You can not fail if you move in the direction of your desire. See the end scene, and feel the feelings if it were so. God will provide the connections, the people and the words for the conversation. Move, take action and see everything's meant to bring you to the end scene result that you have envisioned. Keep this prayer desire between you and God. God will connect you with others that secretly have the same desire or will be players to move your desire into a harvest. When it is manifested in this world of material, you then can give the Glory back to God.

But when you pray, go away by yourself, shut the door behind you, and pray to your Father in private. Then your Father, who sees everything, will reward you.

Matthew 6:6

5

PRAYER

D o you ever think about prayer? Of course, we think about our prayer requests when we are in the act of "praying" or requesting. But have you ever really thought about which of our prayers are answered and which ones are not? Are you one of those that keeps a prayer journal who can look back and see what was answered according to your prayer request?

> ***<u>Do you wonder why some prayers are answered and others are not?</u>***
> ***So shall my word be that goeth forth out of my mouth: it shall not return unto me void, but it shall accomplish that which I please, and it shall prosper in the thing whereto I sent it.***
>
> *Isaiah 55:11 (KJV)*

What if I told you ALL your prayers are being answered? Whether or not you believe God has given unto you, or maybe you believe it's not God's will for you, so he chooses not to allow it to be answered as you had hoped. What if you knew how to determine what God responds to and began to effectively pray for receiving what you are asking God for? Just that last question hopefully gets you a little excited. I have always had the desire to know God, to know His Will, to know he is ALWAYS listening and ALWAYS present. Funny to imagine we are trained to believe God loves us so much, he gave us his only son. But it seems like when we need him, we have to go looking for him. Doesn't that ring any bells that the teaching we receive from the world is really skewed?

I know when I was struggling in my prayer life, I'd wanted to know…if I pray, how do I convince God to make me rich! Skinny? Find the love of my life, you know the person I've chosen, not whom God personally appointed to be that mate? How do I pray to get a better job? Etc, etc…

Well, this next sentence might discourage you a tinch. Now that my prayer life is getting more "predictable," in receiving what I am requesting.

The desire for money, or a particular person to be my mate, a specific job, yadda, yadda, yadda. These requests are no longer important to me. I've discovered it's not my core desire. Yes, I still asked and continually received an abundance of money. I've been able to fully love my wife in ways I never knew how. I've been able to save my marriage and really deeply communicate with my wife. Even though there was a time she was adamant, she was not ever dealing with my unloving and selfish ways. Really I was a pig!

What I discovered within myself when I was just really learning how to pray effectively was to just be happy with the core elements of my desires. I didn't want anything but God. I was hurt and I was broken.

Listen, in NO WAY am I implying don't pray big and expect big or bigger. No, I'm saying with whom my Spirit is, I was just happy to start with, never being worried about money. Being loved and respected, Successful…you see, successful is a blanket desire. So my prayers for success focused daily on what my calendar was for the day. Also, keep in mind, I was moving myself into other mentally visual "States", and what was important and increasing in desire was I wanted the deep closeness with God. I wanted to just believe him and forget about what this world was telling me to believe. It all sounds simple. Trust me, it gets easier when you tune out the noise and control your thoughts. It takes time to eliminate bad habits within the mind. Be glad that it does take effort. So when you achieve this personal power, it won't be easily lost.

He that is faithful in that which is least is faithful also in much: and he who is unjust in what is least is unjust also in much.

LUKE 16:10 (KJV)

I built my prayer life out from there. Starting basic for me, this was easier for me to build up to my prayer life today. I, like you, will continue to evolve and grow. Not as this man your eyes can see, but as who I really am. Spirit. Fulfilling my purpose within this garment known to the world as "man", others know as Todd. Being a Creator is my real purpose in this life of death.

Our Prayers are our reality. Our lives, as seen by man, are only a shadow, a reflection of our secret prayers and our thoughts. When we are praying, we are focusing our thoughts on the solution of our desire. Seeking Jesus to be our Savior. Prayer is seeing the end. Understand we are continually in prayer. This is the key, *but we are not continually focused* on our prayers and our desires. This focus is the difference between having the life and the experiences that you want and desire. Or just getting life and not fulfilling our desires, so we just accept what life gives us.

How should you pray? Let me suggest it's exactly the way I do. I only suggest "How you should pray" as the way I do because to me, it is proven to honor the law by the results I am getting. You bought this book to get the results you desire. Follow, track, measure, and be mindful of the dedication and focus it takes. You're having to overcome a lifelong habit of letting your thoughts and feelings rule you. You have to overcome the world.

Guard your heart above all else, for it determines the course of your life.

Proverbs 4:23 (NLT)

For as he thinketh in his heart, so is he

Proverbs 23:7 (KJV)

I have told you all this so that you may have peace in me. Here on earth you will have many trials and sorrows. But take heart, because I have overcome the world.

John 16:33

I want to discuss feelings 1st. For the longest time, I never understood what was being asked of me to feel. My personality is rarely high or low, so to get excited about much is very difficult for me.

When you have a desire, whether it's a good or bad desire, you feel an emotional change. Begin to notice when your thoughts come on with force. If you slow it down, you will notice the feeling comes 1st. This is where the thoughts enter your mind. The feeling is the secret. Control your feelings, and you will begin to have control of your thoughts.

Let me ask you, how would you feel if you met the most amazing person while you're single and looking for a mate? Ask yourself how you would feel if your spending money were low and you were now late on a payment? How would you feel if somebody gave you the money to cover this late payment? How would you feel if you needed to lose a considerable amount of weight and you looked in the mirror and it was gone?

And hope does not put us to shame, because God's love has been poured into our hearts through the Holy Spirit who has been given to us.

Romans 5:5 (ESV)

But the Helper, the Holy Spirit, whom the Father will send in my name, he will teach you all things and bring to your remembrance all that I have said to you.

John 14:26 (ESV)

Likewise the Spirit helps us in our weakness. For we do not know what to pray for as we ought, but the Spirit himself intercedes for us with groanings to deep for words.

Romans 8:26 (ESV)

When the Spirit of truth comes, he will guide you into all truth, for he will not speak on his own authority, but whatever he hears he will speak, and he will declare to you the things that are to come.

John 16:13 (ESV)

This feeling is the spark. This is the heart in action. This is the Holy Spirit. Recognize the good feelings that are fruitful, and then practice finding this feeling at will through the imagination of your desires. Get skilled at how to find and emit this feeling at will. The more intense, the quicker you will cross that bridge into the answered prayer or desire. I'm not asking you to daydream or folly to feel the feelings of your desires. No, I'm telling you, you have enough desires constantly that are your cues to move in that particular direction.

Get the feeling of your desire. Big or small. Most are small. That's OK. Small reaps bigger rewards in the Kingdom of God. And move towards taking the action of completing. See the end result. How do you feel at the end of the day if you move from success to success to success?

Feels good, doesn't it? Now move! Don't worry about the steps to take, the people to meet, the places to go. The Holy Spirit will guide you, and God will give you the words. God will impress upon you the next action. Don't get bogged down with the "HOW". Just move on to your desire. Consider your desire as an unwritten goal. Write it down if you need. Trust God will move you to hit targets that move in the direction of fulfilling the desire or goal.

Your sin will not be completing the desire. It's not what the world tells you "sin" is. Yes, the Bible has many references to what you should not do. Is it possible that what man says is God's sin? Is God giving you instruction to not lose your mind and your thoughts to this world? I see some of the "sins" man has listed as a man trying to dominate man. God gave you your Spirit and your life in this world. God is always

I believe because God tells us. God is Love. God is peace. God is good. God is the truth. God is mercy. God will not be mocked. A biblical reference says Mockers, also called scoffers in scripture, defy and renounce truth and good things, not only to their own detriment and destruction but to that of others. Realize and do not doubt there still is "truth" in evil. To turn from these thoughts and feelings, turn and find love and peace. Controlling your mind and thoughts is a choice. Not an easy choice, but not impossible. You can break yourself free of destructive thought habits. One thought at a time. Practice seizing your thoughts by just stopping thoughts and directing your mind to what is good. We all struggle.

Finally, brethren, whatsoever things are true, whatsoever things are honest, whatsoever things are just, whatsoever things are pure, whatsoever things that are lovely, whatsoever things are of good report; if there be any virtue, and if there be any praise, think on these things.

Philippians 4:8 (KJV)

Let's be clear on what I'm talking about with desire. This is a pretty basic example, but I believe you'll see it for what it really is. When you're hungry, well, your desire is to eat something. It's not what you eat that you desire, it's a relief of the hunger pangs that are now your every thought and is the relief you are seeking. If you are very sick, you only want to be well. You're not thinking about how or what medicine will make you well. You just desire to be well. In desire, we just want the end result. We want the outcome.

I recommend using a Prayer Journal, or a Desire Book. Within these writings I keep my desires. I, at times, document even the smallest of desires. Mind you, a desire is not something you want. Really we all pretty much want a million dollars, great health, a sensual loving relationship sharing a life of adventure. It's not wrong to want any of these and more. When you can differentiate your desire from your wants. You are attentive to God's word directly to you, "desire" vs. your free will. Don't let anyone tell you what God is saying to you. God may use another to say or do something that confirms the conversation with him. But nobody but God can speak directly to your Spirit. He created you, the plans he has for us, and most importantly your Spirit he created in his image.

For I know the plans I have for you, says the Lord. They are plans for good and not for disaster, to give you a future and hope.

Jeremiah 29:11 (NLT)

So God created human beings in his own image. In the image of God he created them; male and female he created them.

Genesis 1:27 (NLT)

You can, and many more do achieve their free will. Only to feel complete in the act of achievement of such, but empty, unfulfilled, a void or emotionally lost outside of this freewill. Freewill used to feel like a double-edged sword to me. If I did only what I wanted, the way I wanted to accomplish something, I would always have this unfillable void in my life. If I did what I was told by religious scholars and society, exactly what they believed God wanted and expected of me, well, like you, I could never measure up. Others, it appeared, were being blessed with "the good life" as I was destined to be a living martyr for God in every sense….struggle with financial resources, my relation-ships, owning dependable vehicles, etc, etc…hopefully, you get the gist of what I'm saying. You call on God by imagining the achieved desire and how you would feel if so. This is where you get to our Father, our super subconscious mind, through Jesus and the act of imag-ining the end result of the desire. Don't doubt the thoughts and promptings you are receiving, moving towards the fulfillment of the desire. Don't question how God is arranging the outside world, bringing the fulfillment of your desire.

Just as you cannot understand the path of the wind or the mystery of a tiny baby growing in its mother's womb, so you cannot understand the activity of God, who does all things.

Ecclesiastes 11:5 (NLT)

Daydreaming is not a desire. Daydreams are not productive and will waste your time, your talents, and the ability to seek out God's Will. Get control of your daydreams and focus your thoughts on your real desires. Once you can isolate a desire, put your prayers, your thought of thinking, imagining the end result, what it looks like achieved. Once you manage this and combine it with how you'd feel if true, don't revisit it again. Don't question or even think about how God will make it appear or manifest. That's not your concern.

Commit your actions to the Lord, and your plans will succeed.

Proverbs 16:3 (NLT)

When you begin to isolate your desires from the noise of the world. Worry not because God will reveal more and more desires. You won't run out, nor will you not have anything to do. You always have to get out to be with others and get up from your isolation. Begin to talk to others, get out of the house. Pick up the phone and call. Let God bring forth the people necessary to bring the desire into manifestation. Many times to me my desires are bringing what to the world as a negative event. In reality, I see it as God pruning my life and my situation to make way for the end manifestation. God loves to perform miracles. Why wouldn't he? He performs so many of them. He loves what the world tells us verbally, or by looking at a situation, it'll never work out. If you refuse to hear this and see this, you will be watching a miracle unfold. Thank God for hearing you.

"You don't have enough faith," Jesus told them. "I tell you the truth, if you had faith even as small as a mustard seed, you could say to this mountain, 'Move from here to there,' and it would move. Nothing would be impossible."

Matthew 17:20 (NIV)

Don't be afraid, for I am with you. Don't be discouraged, for I am your God. I will strengthen you and help you. I will hold you up with my victorious right hand.

Isaiah 41:10 (NLT)

6
FAITH

Faith is quite simply stated, To believe in receiving something without proof or requesting to give another, without first seeing it, touching it, or understanding it. That, at some time, it will be realized.

Now faith is the substance of things hoped for, the evidence of things not seen.

Hebrews 11:1 (KJV)

I keep having to remind myself I'm not writing this book to teach you what you can learn on your own.

Understanding how I want you to interpret the last sentence is only by what you can learn when you are reading the Bible. God will speak to you in ways outside of the Bible. The Bible is the spring you drink from. You then can apply the techniques written on these pages.

I'm writing to share my experience, what God has revealed to me. Exactly how I apply the Spiritual Law, how God began to interpret the Bible to me. God has laws that he does not waiver on. God is no respecter of man. God, and you, are spirit. You're flesh and free will move about this world. A world your spirit does not and will not be ultimately consumed by. You came from God, and you will return to God. God wants you to know and accept the great power that is within each of us now. Maybe he speaks to you the same, and like me, you struggle with other religious teachers' interpretation of God's word. When you accept the teachings of others as to who you really are and where God, Jesus, Holy Spirit and Heaven is…you are lost and succumb to the ways of this world. Harsh words, but I say not in judgment of you or others, but myself for failing to follow God completely. When you realize who God and Jesus are and where they are in relation to your free will and movement on this earth. Following them becomes easier than sitting through any Sunday sermon.

Maybe you are like I was. Believing the teachings of other faith leaders. It always boiled down to my actions were something I was doing negatively to myself, and ultimately for the failure to live the life I always knew I should be. They were right by being wrong in their teaching. Yes, I was doing something wrong. I was following them, the religious teachers, to look for God and Jesus and the Holy Spirit somewhere outside of me.

They teach God and or Jesus will come to you. They repeat the Holy Spirit will guide you and lead you in the direction of God's Will. I'm going to start early and not lead up to the truth, God, Jesus, and the Holy Spirit are not coming. You don't have to be "good" to have them show love to you. Or have them respond to you. Continue reading. I'll explain in hopefully a way that will turn on a light in you. Give you control over every area of your life. Strengthen your relationship with the Trinity. Make it so clear by your own testing that you, as the Bible teaches, are never to stop praying. Sounds hard. Sounds tedious. Sounds like another area you would make yourself believe you fall short from God and his blessings. Or God's miracles. Don't believe it! You already are continually praying. You just aren't praying for what you consciously want. But your prayers are always being heard AND always being answered.

Always be joyful. Never stop praying. Be thankful in all circumstances. For this is God's Will for you who belong to Jesus Christ.

Thessalonians 5:16-18 (NLT)

Really it Boils down to the simplest elements. It is faith. It is a feeling. What you choose to believe. What you choose to feel. The fact is, whether you realize it or not, we all believe in something. And everyone of us begins to think, first by the way we feel. Slow it down. You'll realize your thoughts begin with a feeling you have, an emotion, if you will. So the secret isn't in strictly training your mind through repetition of feel good mantras. No, you must realize your feelings are a choice. It may be by a habit, but you are choosing to feel the way you do. Choose to feel good about yourself. People you know. People in general. The work you do.

Yes, we do have layers and layers of hard feelings. Which gives us the thoughts of fear, anger, love, hate, and you can name it. If it is possible to feel emotional, we feel it. What I do is rewrite in my thoughts what I don't want to feel terrible about anymore. The act of revision.

Then Peter came to him and asked, "Lord, how often should I forgive someone who sins against me? Seven times?"

"No, not seven times," Jesus replied, "but seventy times seven!"

Matthew 18:21-22 (NLT)

I rewrite those events, conversations, and experiences that were not pleasing to me. It's my thoughts, and I have the right to control them and my feelings. I go back and replay these thoughts in my mind. I rethink them. They now play out how I wanted them to be. The words I wanted to be said by another. I play it over and over until it just feels good to think about. Then I embrace or handshake the other people in my thoughts and say to myself through words, "it is finished". I then thank my Father for hearing me. Finally, I let it go and refuse to revisit in my mind any thought that isn't what I just rewrote in my mind. When I have revised a negative thought and feeling, I don't struggle with it appearing in my thoughts again. If it does randomly show up, I immediately go back to my revision. Quickly, that good and loving feeling I wanted appears, and the thought is gone. It's only as hard as you allow it to be.

...that ye may be the children of your Father which is in Heaven: for he maketh his sun to rise on the evil and the good, and sendeth rain on the just and on the unjust.

Matthew 5:45 (KJV)

Faith or the thought of what isn't seen but we are afraid of seeing, and the poor feeling that starts the thought is heard by God. It does not matter if it is good or bad. If this is where you put your faith, these are the seeds you sow and, ultimately, the harvest you will reap. It's worth stating this again: Faith is quite simply stated, To believe in receiving something without proof or requesting to give another, without first seeing it, touching it, understanding it. That, at some time, it will be realized.

When you begin the act of imagining what you want AND what you don't want, you are always in accordance with God's law. I will say this a thousand times if need be, God is no respecter of man. Your thoughts become God's word, and they will not come back void.

7

STATES

A question I asked myself when I became aware of "mental states". What is a "State," and how do I use it? I began to wonder exactly how does a "State" affect me?

A State is a vision you see in your mind. Before I expand on this, I want you to see if you can relate with me. I've always had big dreams or ideas that I perceived in my thoughts, popping up so clearly in my mind. I've always believed in God. I'm not eluding; you must believe in God to experience the same. I myself have always been influenced by the preaching of the times. My earliest recollection was when I was a young boy. At that tender age, I would follow those that were taller than I, that I believed really did have all the answers, unfailable.

God, in my earliest remembrance of religious teaching, was always outside of me. Jesus Christ was outside of me. After being risen from death after being hung on the cross, Jesus disappeared to only be soon seen when he decided to come back in the clouds for all of us Christians walking the earth. This event could or could not be in my lifetime. Obviously, Jesus's return, and the rapture, taught by modern Christian teaching, weren't timed for my ancestors before me. And I'm sure they were waiting and watching like I have been.

Now the vivid thoughts I was having didn't ring a bell inside of me until one day sitting in a small church in Ordway, Colorado. The preacher who was preaching to be the best of the day and times preaching brimstone and hell. You know, preaching God's love. This "faith leader" brought all people into his sermon, Ozzy Osbourne. Wow! That was the day I was forever changed. The day I began to question. The day I began to seek. Not from man, but God himself.

I won't be fooled. God does use man to speak to us. Also, understand God uses many, many things to show us he's real. He's here. He hears us and loves us. God uses every opportunity not only to speak to us but prove to us his unfailing faith, hope, and love. Discernment is hearing what moves you to accomplish your desires. Just about everything else is noise.

The Heavens proclaim the glory of God. The skies display his craftsmanship. Day after day they continue to speak; night after night they make him known. They speak without sound or word; their voice is never heard.

Psalms 19:1-3 (NLT)

For God speaks again and again, though people do not recognize it.

Job 33:14 (NLT)

The State of mind I can illustrate by getting you to see the room or space you are in now. Look around, really see what you're seeing. Not only are you seeing, but you are experiencing the expression or manifestation of your thoughts, the seeds you planted who knows when. You now are thinking and building later today, tomorrow, or who knows when from this space, this room. Your thoughts yesterday, last week, or whenever you were thinking from this space. You are not thinking ABOUT this space, this room, you are thinking FROM. This space or room is the image projected from what STATE you are thinking from. Unless you think from a different state and not about it, then this is the state of mind you will remain.

When you pray, you enter into the desired State. You are imagining what it looks like, feels like, sounds like. Your thoughts are your prayers. Your desire is the

Word of God. Feel what it would feel like, and you have married the State of thought and feeling to give birth to the manifestation of the desire. Your faith, which in simplicity what you are believing is true to pass, will bring it to pass.

> *Rejoice always, pray without ceasing, give thanks in all circumstances; for this is the will of God in Christ Jesus for you.*
>
> *Thessalonians 5:16-18 (ESV)*

When you enter this elevated State, your thoughts should elevate, and think from here. You are not becoming this person. No, you are being this person. You must, you must not be double-minded.

> *A double-minded man is unstable in all his ways.*
>
> *James 1:8 (KJV)*

God helps us understand by telling us not to look back. You don't have to forget, as a man, I haven't been instructed how not to. It's been said that forgiveness is forgetting all the transgressions. Am I there forgetting…no, never.. I am letting go of the pain or the emotion it caused. I am forgiving. More so for me, but the love is for both.

Then Peter came to him and asked, "Lord, how often should I forgive someone who sins against me? Seven times?"
"No, not seven times," Jesus replied, "but seventy times seven!"

Matthew 18:21-22 (NLT)

Where I struggled. Only because I thought I had to force something, I thought I had to force anything. I had to force the thoughts, I had to force the actions. No. God tells us to give it to him. I trust him. I give it to God. I urge you to do the same.

Be still, and know that I am God: I will be exalted among the heathen, I will be exalted in the earth.

Psalm 46:10 (KJV)

8

STRUGGLING WITH THE LAW

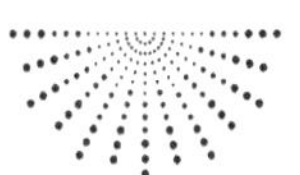

Since 1st learning and beginning to practice the law, I've been having good success. For what others may think are "little" things. I ignore it because I'm not interested in the thoughts or opinions of others about or what is concerning my journey in this life. And neither should you. This life is my gift from God. Only he and I should determine how it is lived concerning me. Thus this is between you and God the same. Your personal relationship and awareness.

Over this time of testing the law, I've been having great sales in business, strangers are being nicer and more respectful. I even tried to have somebody contact me, whom I know of, but we don't really know each other. As a matter of fact, we've never met in person. For this test I selected this person solely on the amount of time that had transpired from a 5-minute casual conversation many months prior.

When they contacted me, though not surprised, I was in amazement at how easily the law was applied and returned to me. The lesson to learn from this is not that it worked for me. No, the law is continually working for me. It never stops. Before the law was revealed to me, it brought me more of what I didn't want.

Now I've proven to myself, it brings me more of what I do want. My takeaway is always recognizing EVERYTHING is unfolding to answer your prayers. Your desires are your prayers. Even what seems to be negative or failures is just God pruning from your current mental state. Recognize these so as not to look back on them as normal or acceptable.

Let me point out, I myself have put myself into another mental "State". I do this by not thinking about the mental state, I fulfill it by thinking from this mental state.

I do my very best to continually speak my desires multiple times a day. Not like a mantra, but in the form "I Am." We are to believe and drop the petition knowing in faith it is done. I do, and I have. Repeating my desire quietly in private throughout the day, for me, is not doubting. It is more and more training me for recognizing God arranging my life by always answering my prayers. This is keeping me focused on accepting his rearrangement in any way that is necessary for living fruitfully in the desired mental state. I don't question how God provides and arranges. I accept the work, the conversations that are in front of me.

No, I repeat my prayers because, like you, I need to build that spiritual muscle for when Satan, or doubt, confusion, or fear, whatever you're comfortable calling it, tries to snap me back into the mental state I've elevated from. That was, for me, the mental state for the lack in everything. I've come to learn how we react, and this reaction will reveal our current state.

And you will know the truth, and the truth will set you free.

John 8:32 (NLT)

Another thing I've noticed is I've turned off the radio unless it's Classic Rock or Contemporary Christian...I know, that's one heckuva swing in the musical genre. Really though, Classic Rock takes my senses back to when I truly believed I ruled the world...before I began sweeping the streets...Contemporary Christian music is soothing because others are praising God and, of course, the actual talent of the vocalist and musicians. Really though, for me, it gets harder and harder to listen to. Only because the lyrics in many songs want to point to a God or Jesus Christ outside of me...as though I've got to find him somewhere and elude Heaven is outside of me.

The reason we struggle and everyone does and will. Breaks Down to the simplest cause. We've trained ourselves to follow the rules OR expectations. Either personally, societally, religiously, family, or culturally. You name it, and there is a rule or expectation to follow. Almost all outside of scripture. Our misfortune is that we tend to hold the man-made rules closer than the Word of God.

These rules and expectations are all tied to an undesired self-imposed punishment or a negative thought. You miss the slightest of any worldly learned rule or expectation, and the self prison sentence begins.

Start by removing all rules, punishments, and guilt from your mind. This includes stress from having to get things. How this is accomplished, you may be asking. What you are about to read sounds easy. Applying the technique becomes difficult consistently. Not impossible. Difficult.

Like a trained athlete or dancer, with exercise and repetition it becomes natural. When they're working their body, they become mindful of the form they are practicing. The diet and liquids they are consuming. The concept will not be difficult, quieting and controlling the noise right now in your head will be the challenge.

Here is the 1st door…You accomplish removing the

impediments written above by simply thinking you want the freedom to think this way. Freedom is free of personal restrictions and expectations. Nobody knows what you're thinking, what you're giving up on. What you are pruning from your mind. Releasing the chains and shackles that hold you back. I doubt it, but you may think they may assume you're giving up on restrictions and worldly expectations adopted by others, but never mind them. Just as you don't worry or think what others are thinking. It's none of your kingdom's business.

Everyday, many, many times in a day, sometimes many times within the hour. I, too, struggle with the thoughts that condemn me. I catch myself, really come on, you just like I know when a thought that just brought on feelings of anguish or many forms of negativity in your thoughts. When you catch yourself going here. It has become so natural, it seems to be the bulk of your own inner conversations. So catch it once. And think, ask yourself, "where are these thoughts taking place?"

Well, obviously, and you'll see the simple answer to your own question. They are within me. I created them. So if I can create them, I can just as simply, and this is really the easy part, the key to unlock the door to freedom, I can change them. Or I can completely rid of them.

Nevertheless, though I write these words, I struggle with the application. I can encourage you. It does get easier with utilizing the application and the struggle on "not believing". I come back to the basics. Everyone is entitled to their own thoughts. I recognize it is the state where they exist. I instinctively want to pass judgment. But judgment is not mine.

> ***Judge not, that ye be judged. For with that judgment ye judge, ye shall be judged: and with that measure ye mete, it shall be measured to you again.***
>
> *Matthew 7:1-2 (KJV)*